Appliqué at Play
19 Sports Blocks to Mix and Match

DeElda Wittmack

Martingale ®
& C O M P A N Y

Appliqué at Play: 19 Sports Blocks to Mix and Match
© 2006 by DeElda Wittmack

That Patchwork Place® is an imprint of
Martingale & Company®.

Martingale & Company
20205 144th Avenue NE
Woodinville, WA 98072-8478 USA
www.martingale-pub.com

Credits

President: Nancy J. Martin
CEO: Daniel J. Martin
COO: Tom Wierzbicki
Publisher: Jane Hamada
Editorial Director: Mary V. Green
Managing Editor: Tina Cook
Technical Editor: Nancy Mahoney
Copy Editor: Ellen Balstad
Design Director: Stan Green
Illustrator: Robin Strobel
Cover and Text Designer: Shelly Garrison
Photographer: Brent Kane

Printed in China
11 10 09 08 07 06   8 7 6 5 4 3 2 1

Library of Congress Cataloging-in-Publication Data
Library of Congress Control Number: 2006020427

ISBN-13: 978-1-56477-698-3
ISBN-10: 1-56477-698-0

Mission Statement

Dedicated to providing quality products and service to inspire creativity.

Dedication

To Penny, who started this sewing thing with me at age 13
To Joyce, who doesn't sew anything—thank goodness

Acknowledgments

There are many people who have helped me iron my way through this lifelong love affair with fabric, and I would like to thank them.

Virginia Kurtz, who passed away in 2004 at age 93, was the owner of The Roosevelt Fabric Shop in Des Moines, Iowa, for many years. She gave me my first job, was very tough, and taught me everything there was to know about fabric. Her daughter, Carolyn Kurtz Hosier, has been a friend and neighbor and has always shared her love of quilting with me. She and my Iowa friend in Honolulu, Dwyta Schroeder, have the best color sense of any quilters I have ever known, and I truly appreciate them and their talents.

Ruth Smith and Margaret Sindelar are two friends who have always been there to answer quilting questions and to quickly sew anything and everything I have given them. Ruth always makes time to fabric shop with me, and her cheerfulness for each project is wonderful. Margaret's late-night encouragement as I worked on this book has kept me going. Thank you both.

There are many others without whom I could not have created this book. Connie Dorn and all her helpers at Creekside Quilting in West Des Moines have been very supportive. Patty Barrett, you are my idol!

I would also like to thank the wonderful people at Martingale & Company who promised me the book would look great and were right. Mary Green, Ellen Balstad, Terry Martin, and Nancy Mahoney are the magicians who helped bring my concept to fruition.

Thank you, one and all! We have done this together.

Contents

Introduction

As a designer of handcrafts and needlework for more years than I wish to count, I've been amazed at the lack of printed design material for the sports enthusiasts among us. Therein lies the reason for this book. Practically *everyone* has at least one sports nut in the family. If you're reading this book, you're probably a quilter and have wished at one time or another that you could incorporate your family's leisure activities with yours by designing a project with a sports theme. And now you can.

Just think about how much fun it would be to make a pillow to remember your daughter's first tennis tournament win. Or perhaps you could make a wall hanging of your family dog, sitting quietly among the fine array of sports equipment outside the back door. And wouldn't it be great to curl up in the "Sports Galore Quilt" (page 38) on a cool Sunday afternoon as the family watches their favorite football team on television?

With a little practice, all these quilted pillows, wall hangings, and quilts are quick and easy to sew with a sewing machine that has a zigzag stitch. Make unique gifts for anyone on your gift list. And, you can finish almost all of the projects in a day or a weekend.

With this book, you'll also learn about painting on fabric. I'll show you the technique for painting eyes on animals, as well as other simple tips that will quickly and easily bring out the artist in each one of you.

Whether you want to make a big project to commemorate a lifetime of family fun, or something smaller for an extra-special, one-time performance, this book will help you get started. So come along and express your own creativity while quilting a memory. You may be surprised at what you can do—but I won't.

Designs—
Make Them Your Own

I've created 19 block designs that you can mix and match to make any of the projects in this book. The original design blocks are listed for each project. You can follow the basic instructions for the project while substituting any of the design blocks with others you may prefer. To personalize the blocks, you'll be enlarging, reducing, adding, or deleting elements within each block, which adds to the fun. If you're a more traditional quilter and prefer to hand appliqué your project, go for it. Just add a ¼" seam allowance around each element before cutting the shape.

Of the 19 block designs, 15 are sporting motifs. The other four are a dog, a cat, a kite, and a star—because pets are wonderful, kites are fun on a windy day, and sports teams and parents always have a star in their midst. One clever use of the star design is as a nameplate. On a larger quilt, you may have several stars to represent members of a group. Most names should fit, but if you have a very long name, fatten the star in the middle. Just trace the design, extending the middle out a little. Of course, you can use nicknames, monograms, or initials. Try to be consistent if you have several stars in one project.

Names and words can be embroidered by hand or by machine. Some of you may have sewing machines that do this type of embroidery. You can often find businesses that do machine embroidery listed in the phone book under "Embroidery." If there is no listing, call a local uniform shop or a sports store that embroiders names on uniforms for local teams. They are a good source of information, even if they are not able to help you with the embroidery.

To give you options when designing your own projects, I've included different versions of the same thing, such as multiple suns and moons, or blocks that have grass and blocks that don't. Choose your favorite details and leave some off altogether. Remember—you're the designer. The technique for moving things around and designing your own block is simple. On a large piece of tracing paper, draw a square outline the finished size of your block. On a separate piece of tracing paper, trace the design elements you'd like to have in the block. Cut out the elements and arrange them in a design that is pleasing to *you*. Finally, trace your finished design block to make a pattern.

Enlarging and reducing the design on a copy machine is fun, easy, and very rewarding. The results are often surprising, and the possibilities are endless. When creating your own design, try several different percentage settings when enlarging or reducing. Sometimes a 5% change can make a big difference. Once you have the size you like, cut the design elements from the paper and arrange them on your drawn square. Then trace your finished design block to make a pattern.

Painting on Fabric

Painting on fabric is fun and easy to do, and it is a technique that will set your work apart from the others. I often use paint to make the eyes of animals on quilts. There are button eyes and plastic, movable "googly" eyes from craft shops, but I prefer to paint more realistic eyes on my very unrealistic cats and dogs. I've listed the few tools you'll need below:

- Fabric paint such as Delta Ceramcoat in Black, White, Brown, and Green for the projects in this book

- Brushes (I use Loew-Cornell) in size 00 for tiny detail work and size 01 for slightly larger areas

- Scraps of fabric on which to practice

- Paper towel to put under your work

- Fusible web

- Quilter's permanent archival fine-tipped pen

If you are appliquéing the painted eye, enlarge it slightly from the drawing in the block. Use a quilter's permanent pen and trace the eye as shown. Paint the iris circle in brown for a dog and green for a cat. After this is dry, paint a straight line down the middle of the eye with black, and then curve the middle outward in a slight arc. The last thing to add is a white dot to bring your animal to life. If the animal has only one eye showing, put the dot anywhere within the arc of black. If the animal has two eyes showing, place the white dots on either the left or right side of both arcs so that the animal does not look cross-eyed.

After the paint has dried overnight, iron fusible web to the back of the fabric and cut out the eye, leaving a seam allowance the approximate width of the zigzag stitch you are using around the outline of the eye. The seam allowance will be covered with a machine satin stitch, so when you finish sewing, the eye will be perfect.

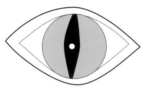

Appliqué margin around eye.

When appliquéing a very small animal, paint the eye directly on the fabric of the animal. For example, a fish just has a round little eye, which is very easy to paint.

The hockey skate design is another place to practice your painting. You can add real eyelets for the skate, but you can also paint them. While experimenting in my studio, I grabbed a quilter's permanent pen and noticed that the top of the cap looked just like an eyelet. After I mixed up a little gray paint (white with a little black added), I dipped the cap into the paint, and presto, the eyelets were on the hockey skate.

Once you've tried painting on fabric, you'll be hooked and perhaps continue to look for places where you can test your new skill. Have fun playing with paint.

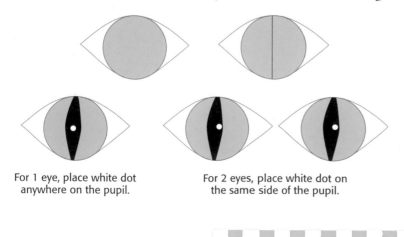

For 1 eye, place white dot anywhere on the pupil.

For 2 eyes, place white dot on the same side of the pupil.

Techniques to Make You an Expert

Everyone needs refreshers now and then, and the following are just that. If you've been quilting for some time, read these helpful hints. You may find something you haven't tried before. If appliqué is new to you, study the appliqué instructions and practice. Have fun and good luck.

TOOLS FOR PROJECTS

There are many wonderful tools available to the home quilter. Before you begin designing your projects with the help of this book, you should have most of the following on hand:

- A good sewing machine with a zigzag stitch
- Scissors used only for fabric
- Light box—my personal favorite tool
- Rotary cutter, cutting mat, and rulers
- Seam ripper
- Quilter's permanent archival fine-tipped pen
- Water-soluble marker
- Lightweight fusible web
- Lightweight, tear-away stabilizer
- Lightweight batting (80% cotton and 20% polyester works beautifully for hand or machine quilting)
- Selection of good-quality cotton threads
- Fabric paints and brushes for painting eyes, listed in "Painting on Fabric" on page 6

ACCURATE SEAM ALLOWANCES

Perhaps the most important quiltmaking skill to perfect is the ability to stitch consistent seam allowances when piecing two fabrics together. Unless specified otherwise, always use a ¼"-wide seam allowance.

Some sewing machines have a special quilting presser foot that measures exactly ¼" from the center needle position to the edge of the foot. This allows you to use the edge of the foot to guide the fabric and to get a perfect ¼" seam allowance. If your machine doesn't have a quilting presser foot, you can create a seam guide by placing a piece of colored tape ¼" from the needle.

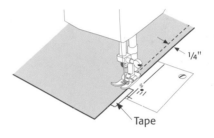

MACHINE APPLIQUÉ

Since this is a book about machine-appliqué designs, I won't go into detail about hand appliqué. The projects in this book can be hand appliquéd, if you choose to do so. For excellent guidance regarding all aspects of hand appliqué, see *The Magic of Quiltmaking: A Beginner's Guide* by Margaret Rolfe and Jenny Bowker (Martingale & Company, 2004). The information that follows is for the beginning machine-appliqué artist.

Using Fusible Web

The technique of fusing designs to a background fabric is quick, reliable, and very satisfying. The invention of paper-backed fusible web has made machine appliqué quite easy. You just iron the fusible web to the back of your appliqué fabrics, cut the shapes out, and fuse the designs to your background fabric. Later, you'll outline the designs using a satin stitch, which I explain in "Machine-Appliqué Stitch" on page 8.

I prefer a lightweight fusible web. It adheres nicely yet lets me easily machine stitch through the layers. I also like the flexibility that lightweight fusible web gives my finished pieces. And, if I fuse a design in the wrong spot, it will often peel off so that I can reposition it.

While most of my pop-art quilted hangings won't be laundered, the larger bed quilts definitely will be. Whether you wash your fabric before you sew or not (hangings—no, quilts for use—yes), or wash the finished project, the lightweight fusible web should work just fine.

Before fusing the designs to your quilt project, test samples of the materials you're going to use. Remember, fusible web is glue! The fusible web you choose should make the design adhere, but your fabric should not become stiff. If the needle of your machine pulls at the fabric, or becomes sticky from sewing the fusible web, investigate using another brand.

The technique for using fusible web is as follows:

1. Cut a piece of fusible web large enough to trace all the project design elements that use the same fabric. Using a pencil or a fine-tipped quilter's permanent pen, trace the shapes on the paper side of the fusible web. Leave a small amount of space between the shapes for ease of cutting. Cut around the entire area of paper shapes as a group. Use leftover scraps of fusible web for smaller, individual tracings. Note that the designs in this book are shown as the reverse of the finished block.

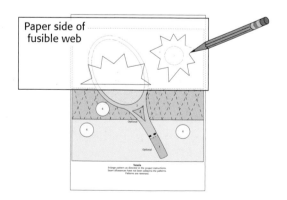

2. Fuse the group of shapes to the wrong side of the appropriate fabric. Cut out each shape on the drawn line.

3. Remove the paper backing and position the shapes on your background fabric. Follow the manufacturer's instructions to fuse the appliqué pieces in place.

Stabilizer: Why Use It?

Stabilizer is a product that is truly magical when it comes to machine appliqué. The needle of the machine goes through the stabilizer with each stitch, evening out the satin stitches beautifully. It's especially helpful when stitching around small areas and tiny inside corners, and for large curves and lines. If you've appliquéd without using stabilizer, I can guarantee you'll notice a difference once you have tried it.

Stabilizers come in all types, weights, and widths. The yardage requirements for the projects in this book are based on 20"-wide stabilizer or packets of 8½" x 11" sheets. To use the stabilizer, cut a piece the required size for the project or individual block on which you're working. Pin the piece of stabilizer under the background fabric of the appliqué design. After stitching around the appliqué shapes, simply turn the design over and gently tear the excess stabilizer off the back. Some stabilizers tear more easily than others, so be careful to remove the stabilizer without pulling or stretching the fabric.

Some of the patterns have details to be stitched within the design. Often the inside design or detail stitching can be done before the piece is fused onto the background fabric; it's easier to manipulate the design area and rotate the design if necessary. When doing this, you can leave the paper-backed fusible web on the design and just pin a piece of stabilizer to the back before you start sewing these details. Remove both the stabilizer and the fusible web paper before you fuse the design to the background.

Machine-Appliqué Stitch

You'll be using a satin stitch on your sewing machine to outline the designs and to add detail. To make a satin stitch, set the machine for a zigzag stitch and a shorter-than-normal stitch length. You'll also want to use a presser foot that allows you to sew a zigzag stitch. If you make the zigzag stitches too close together, they will produce a ridge of stitches. Aim for stitches that are not too open but that don't form so tightly that they overlap. Be sure that your stitches cover the appliqué shape, not the background. It is easy, but it takes a little initial practice. See "Swing to the Left, Swing to the Right—Your Stitches!" below for more tips.

Experiment with your machine until you find the stitch you prefer, and then practice that stitch before you start each project. The width and length of your appliqué stitch may vary with each quilt project, and it may change depending on the detail you wish to achieve.

When machine appliquéing, use a thread that is the same color as the appliqué, or a contrasting color that will make your design stand out more. Often the design dictates the thread color.

Swing to the Left, Swing to the Right—Your Stitches!

If you're just beginning your appliqué experience, you'll find that the way you use your machine and the positioning of the needle as you go around curves and in and out of tight spots is especially important. You'll always be moving the fabric under the foot of your machine, so you need to be loose and think artistic!

As the needle enters the fabric on the right swing of the stitch, it should be just to the outside of the appliqué shape. This will put the left swing of the stitch well into the appliqué shape and hold it securely in place. Once again, experiment to see what your machine will do.

To be sure sharp outer points are well covered, stop the needle down in either the left or right position, lift the presser foot, turn the fabric, lift the needle and position the fabric so that the needle will enter the fabric ready to cover the zigzags already made on the other side of the point. Lower the presser foot and continue stitching.

To make sharp inner corners, stitch slightly into the corner. Stop with the needle down in the left position. Turn the fabric and continue stitching, covering the previous stitching on the inner corner.

After you've practiced these turning techniques a few times, the stopping and starting will become automatic. Don't be discouraged as you begin to learn these tricks. You'll soon become an expert!

Outside corner

Stop with needle down and turn fabric.

Inside corner

Squaring Up the Blocks

After the appliqué is finished, it is time to measure the blocks and make them all the same size by squaring them up. Even if you're not making multiple blocks, a single hanging or lap quilt still needs this technique performed to be sure that the corners are square and to correct any irregularities. I always start with my appliqué blocks or project oversized and then trim them to the correct size.

One of my favorite tools in my studio is my light-box table, and I use it to square up blocks. You can also use a marked cutting mat, but the light-box table has spoiled me because I can see through the fabric to the gridded mat below. Since most of my design blocks have figures in them, the light-box table gives me a little more flexibility when trimming the finished block.

Follow these steps to trim the blocks:

1. Using a gridded, translucent cutting mat over a light-box table, mark the size of your block on the mat, including the seam allowances, with a colorful tape. If you don't have a translucent cutting mat and a light-box table, you can mark the size of your block on a regular cutting mat placed on a table.

2. Place the block over the taped outline. Using a ruler and rotary cutter, trim off any excess fabric that extends beyond the ruler. Rotate the mat 180°, making sure the trimmed edges are still aligned with the tape; trim the remaining two sides.

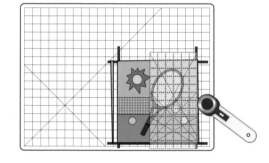

ADDING BORDERS

Borders are always cut to fit the center measurement of the project. Normal stretching of fabric during construction often leaves the side edges a little longer than the center. The measurements for all of the borders in the project instructions are a few inches longer than you will actually need so that you can trim them once you measure the center of your quilt top. If you're a beginning machine-appliqué designer, get into the habit of measuring often so that you won't be disappointed with the results.

All of the projects in this book are designed with straight-sewn corners. The borders will all be sewn in the following way:

1. Measure the length of the quilt through the center. Trim two border strips to that measurement.

2. Mark the centers of the quilt-top sides and the border strips.

Measure top to bottom
through the center.
Mark centers.

3. With the centers matching, sew the borders, easing the fabric if necessary. Press toward the border.

4. Measure the width of the quilt through the center, including the side borders. Cut two strips to that measurement.

5. Mark the center of the top and bottom edges of the quilt top and border strips. Stitch the strips to the top and bottom of the quilt top, matching the centers and ends and easing as necessary.

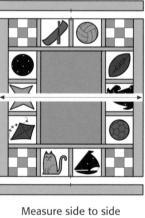

Measure side to side
through the center.
Mark centers.

6. Follow the same technique for additional borders.

FINISHING YOUR QUILT

Completing the final steps for your project is when the sewing of the quilt turns into a joyfest. The finished project is emerging. For this to happen, you need to make a "sandwich" by layering the backing, batting, and quilt top. Then you baste, quilt, and bind. This should be no problem!

Preparing the Backing

The backing is the piece of fabric that will be on the back of your finished project. This can either be the same fabric as your binding, or it can be another complementary fabric of your choosing. The backing should be 4" to 6" larger than your quilt top (2" to 3" on all sides). Often, when making a large quilt such as "Sports Galore Quilt" (page 38), you'll need to piece the backing. Be sure to remove selvages before sewing the pieces together and press the seam allowances open to reduce bulk.

Layering and Basting

Once you complete your quilt top, cut and/or piece your backing, and select your batting, you're ready to baste the three layers together so that they don't shift during the quilting process.

1. Open the package of batting you've chosen, unfold it gently, and allow it to relax overnight.

2. After pressing the backing and the quilt top, spread the backing out, wrong side up, on a clean, flat surface.

3. Use masking tape to hold the backing in place, taking care not to stretch the fabric out of shape. Spread the batting over the backing, making sure it is smooth.

4. Center the pressed quilt top (marked for quilting if you desire), right side up, over the batting. Smooth out any wrinkles and make sure the edges of the quilt top are parallel to the edges of the backing.

5. For hand quilting, baste with needle and thread, starting in the center and working in a grid of horizontal and vertical lines about 6" apart. For machine quilting, baste the layers together using #2 rustproof safety pins. Space the lines and pins for basting about 4" apart. Then baste by hand or machine around the edges about 1/8" from the edge of the quilt top.

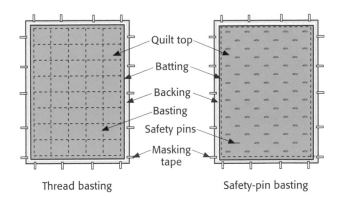

Thread basting   Safety-pin basting

Quilting

Once all your layers are basted together, you can hand or machine quilt as desired. If you don't want to quilt your project, most quilt shops now offer or can refer you to a quilting service. If you'd enjoy learning more about machine quilting, look for the book *Machine Quilting Made Easy!* by Maurine Noble (Martingale & Company, 1994). For excellent guidance regarding all aspects of hand-quilting techniques, see *Loving Stitches: A Guide to Fine Hand Quilting, Revised Edition* by Jeana Kimball (Martingale & Company, 2003)

When the quilting is complete, leave the basting stitches around the edges intact and remove the remaining basting stitches or pins. Trim the batting and backing even with the quilt top. Make sure the corners are square.

Making a Hanging Sleeve

You can add a rod pocket or hanging sleeve to quilts that you wish to hang on the wall. These must be added to the back after you quilt and before you bind the edges. The procedure is quite simple.

1. From leftover backing fabric, cut a piece the width of your quilt and 8" wide. On each end, fold under a 1/2" hem, and then fold under 1/2" again; press and stitch.

2. Fold the strip in half lengthwise, wrong sides together. Stitch 1/4" from the raw edges; press. Center the tube along the back of the quilt, aligning the raw edges with the top edge of the quilt. Baste it in place. Slip-stitch the bottom edge of the sleeve to the backing fabric. When you machine stitch the binding in place, you'll

also stitch the sleeve to the top, hiding the raw edges in the binding.

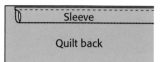

Binding

I use binding strips cut from the straight grain of the fabric to make a double-fold binding that rolls over the edges of the quilt. Cut enough strips to go around the perimeter of your quilt, plus about 10" for making seams and turning corners. The number of strips needed for the binding is included in each project. Once the strips are cut, follow these steps to join the strips and attach the binding.

1. With right sides together, join the strips at right angles and stitch on the diagonal as shown. Trim the excess fabric and press the seam allowances open to make one long piece of binding.

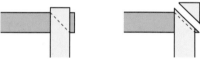

Joining straight-cut strips

2. Fold the strip in half lengthwise, wrong sides together, and press.

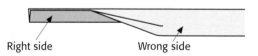

Right side   Wrong side

3. Starting in the middle of one side, align the raw edges of the binding with the quilt top. Leaving the first 8" to 10" of the binding free, stitch the binding to the quilt toward the first corner. End the stitching ¼" from the corner of the quilt and backstitch. Remove the quilt from the machine.

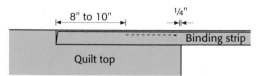

8" to 10"   ¼"
Binding strip
Quilt top

4. Turn the quilt so that you'll be stitching down the next side. Fold the binding away from the quilt so that the fold forms a 45° angle. Then fold the binding back down so that it is even with the next side as shown. Begin stitching at the edge of the binding and continue until you're ¼" from the next corner. Repeat this process at each corner.

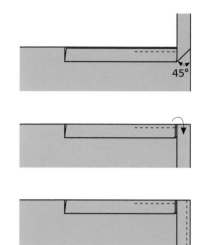

45°

5. Stop sewing about 15" from where you began. Remove the quilt from the machine. Lay the beginning of the binding flat on the quilt top. Overlap the end of the binding over the beginning. Trim the end so that the overlap measures 2½". This overlap should be equal to the width of your binding strip.

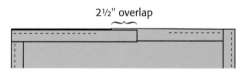

2½" overlap

6. Open and place the strips right sides together, at right angles as shown. Draw a diagonal line and secure the binding with pins.

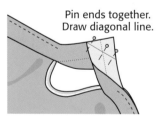

Pin ends together.
Draw diagonal line.

7. Stitch on the diagonal line. Make sure that the joined binding fits before trimming the seam allowance to ¼". Press the seam allowance open.

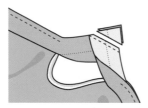

⑧ Refold the binding in half, laying it flat along the quilt edge. Finish sewing the binding to the top.

⑨ Fold the binding over the raw edges of the quilt to the back of the quilt, with the folded edge covering the row of machine stitching. Blindstitch the binding in place. A miter will form at each corner. Blindstitch the mitered corners in place.

Covering Cording

Covered cording creates a line of trim that can be used along the edge of your pillow with or without a ruffle. Uncovered cotton cording is available in most fabric stores. The amount of cording you will need is included in each project, if applicable. To cover the cording, you will need to cut bias strips (strips cut on the diagonal grain of the fabric). The width to cut the strips and the total number of inches needed is also included in each project.

① To make bias strips, use the 45°-angle line on your large cutting ruler as a guide. Cut the strips the width specified in the project.

② Sew the strips together, end to end, and press the seam allowances open.

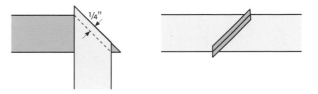

③ To cover the cording, fold the fabric strip in half lengthwise, wrong sides together. Insert the cording, pushing it snugly against the fold.

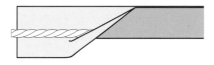

④ Use a zipper foot on your sewing machine and set the needle so that it sews to the left of the foot. Sew the two cut edges of the fabric together, enclosing the cording.

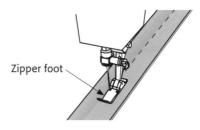

⑤ When you've enclosed the entire piece of cording, trim the seam allowance evenly to ¼".

Adding a Label

A personalized label is a wonderful finishing touch for your quilt. Make the label as plain or interesting as you desire but include your full name, the date, the name of the person you made it for, and anything that you think needs to be remembered. If you use a pen to write the information on the label, iron freezer paper to the back of the fabric to give it stability while you write.

Little Squirt Quilt

Made by DeElda Wittmack. Quilted by Ruth Smith.

The image shows a sailboat appliqué block.

his lap-sized quilt is a fast and easy project to make for a new baby. The simplified design elements could also be used for bumper pads in a crib or a valance over a window in a child's room. Although this quilt was made of regular cotton fabric, soft flannels would also be nice.

The machine-appliqué squares are combined with a simple Nine Patch block in the quilt's primary color of medium blue. The quilt uses 10 different patterns, enlarged and simplified. You could also make it with just a single design element, such as the basketball, sewn in a rainbow of 10 different colors.

Finished Quilt: 36" x 44" ■ Finished Block: 7" x 7"

MATERIALS

All yardages are based on 42"-wide fabric. Fat quarters measure 18" x 21".

2½ yards of green dot print for sashing, border, binding, and backing

⅞ yard of medium blue print for center rectangle and Nine Patch blocks

⅞ yard of white print for appliqué blocks and nine-patch blocks

1 fat quarter of dark blue print for soccer ball and canoe

1 fat quarter of red print for basketball, dog, and sailboat

1 fat quarter of purple print for kite and football

1 fat quarter of dark yellow print for volleyball, star, and cat

40" x 48" piece of batting

1 yard of fusible web

10 sheets, 8½" x 11" (or 1½ yards), of stabilizer

Dark gray thread for appliqué

Fabric paint for animal eyes

CUTTING

All measurements include ¼" seam allowances. Cut all strips across the width of the fabric (selvage to selvage).

From the white print, cut:
10 squares, 8" x 8"
3 strips, 3" x 42"

From the stabilizer, cut:
10 squares, 8" x 8"

From the green dot print, cut:
4 strips, 3" x 42"
5 strips, 2½" x 42"
2 strips, 1½" x 31½"
2 strips, 1½" x 23½"
2 strips, 1½" x 42"; crosscut into 10 rectangles, 1½" x 7½"

From the medium blue print, cut:
1 rectangle, 15½" x 23½"
3 strips, 3" x 42"

For the quilt shown, the designs have been copied at slightly different percentages to fill the 7" blocks. The percentages are different because you have to compensate for the patterns that have multiple design elements; the major element is smaller than it would be by itself. If you were to enlarge all the designs by the same percentage, the designs wouldn't fit into the 7" blocks in a pleasing way. Listed below are the sizes of the individual design elements for each appliqué block. These are subject to personal preference, but keep in mind the relative sizes of the sports equipment you're showing. You may prefer a certain design to be a little larger or smaller within the 7" block, or you may wish to include more of the design elements from the original pattern. The sizes are as follows:

- Football—Enlarge 120% to measure 7½" long.

- Dog—Enlarge 116% to measure 6½" tall.

- Cat—Enlarge 116% to measure 5½" tall.

- Canoe—Enlarge 135% to measure 7⅜" long.

- Volleyball—Enlarge 119% to measure 5¼" in diameter.

- Basketball—Enlarge 119% to measure 5¼" in diameter.

- Sailboat—Enlarge 116% to measure 5¾" tall.

- Kite—Enlarge 116% to measure 6¾" tall.

- Star—Enlarge 116% to measure 6" wide.

- Soccer ball—Enlarge 113% to measure 5" in diameter.

APPLIQUÉING THE BLOCKS

The block patterns for this project are on pages 45–63. Enlarge each pattern to the size mentioned in "D's Tip" at left or until it fits nicely into the 7" design square.

1. Refer to "Machine Appliqué" on page 7 to make the appliqué shapes and apply them to the 8" white print squares. Use the patterns as a layout guide.

2. Pin an 8" square of stabilizer to the back of each block before starting to machine appliqué. Refer to "Stabilizer: Why Use It?" on page 8 as needed.

3. Machine appliqué around each shape. Refer to the photo on page 14 and the pattern for adding details to the individual elements within each block.

4. Paint the animal eyes and let them dry. Refer to "Painting on Fabric" on page 6 as needed. Cut out the painted eye, leaving a seam allowance around each eye. Appliqué the painted animal eyes to the appropriate animal shape.

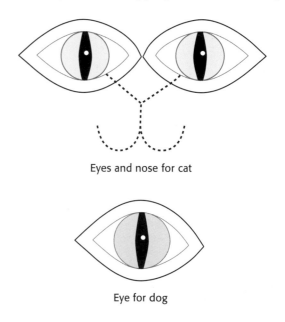

Eyes and nose for cat

Eye for dog

5. For the kite-tail ties, arrange four ¼" x 1½" rectangles and tack in place with several satin stitches, leaving the ends free.

6. Gently remove the stabilizer from the back of the appliqué blocks.

NINE PATCH BLOCKS

1. Sew one 3" x 42" white print strip between two 3" x 42" blue print strips as shown to make strip set A. Cut the strip set into eight 3"-wide segments.

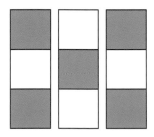

Strip set A.
Make 1. Cut 8 segments.

2. Sew one 3" x 42" blue print strip between two 3" x 42" white print strips as shown to make strip set B. Cut the strip set into four 3"-wide segments.

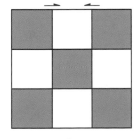

Strip set B.
Make 1. Cut 4 segments.

3. Sew one strip set B segment between two strip set A segments as shown; press. Make four Nine Patch blocks.

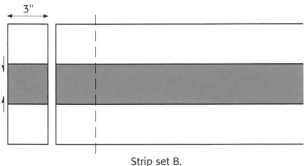

Make 4.

ASSEMBLING THE QUILT TOP

1. Trim the 10 appliqué blocks and the four Nine Patch blocks to 7½" square. Refer to "Squaring Up the Blocks" on page 9 as needed.

2. Sew a 1½" x 23½" green dot strip to each long side of the 15½" x 23½" blue rectangle.

3. Arrange and sew two 1½" x 7½" green dot strips and three appliqué blocks together to make a block row. Be sure to keep the designs facing in the same direction as shown. Press all seams toward the green strips. Make 2. The block rows should measure 7½" x 23½".

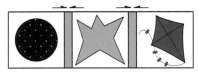

Make 2.

4. Sew a block row from step 3 to each side of the unit from step 2. Be sure to keep the designs facing outward as shown. Press toward the green strips.

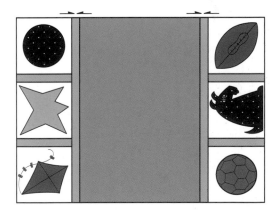

5. Arrange and sew three 1½" x 7½" green dot strips, two appliqué blocks, and two Nine Patch blocks together as shown on page 18 to make a block row. Make two block rows, one for the top and one for the bottom. Be sure to

keep the designs facing in the same direction. Press toward the green strips. The block row should measure 7½" x 31½".

6 Sew a 1½" x 31½" green dot strip to the top of each block row from step 5. With the designs facing outward and the green strips aligned vertically, sew a block row to the top and bottom of the quilt top. Press toward the green strips.

ADDING THE BORDERS

For detailed instructions, refer to "Adding Borders" on page 10.

1 Measure the quilt through the center from top to bottom and trim two 3"-wide green dot border strips to fit that measurement.

2 Sew the trimmed border strips to the side edges of the quilt top. Press toward the border strips.

3 Measure the quilt through the center from side to side, including the borders just added. Trim the remaining 3"-wide green dot border strips to fit that measurement.

4 Sew the trimmed border strips to the top and bottom edges of the quilt top; press.

Quilt assembly

FINISHING THE QUILT

Refer to "Finishing Your Quilt" on page 10 for details on quilt finishing if needed.

1 Cut and piece, if needed, the backing fabric so that it is approximately 4" to 6" larger than the quilt top. Layer the quilt top with batting and backing. Baste the layers together.

2 Hand or machine quilt as desired. You may wish to quilt in the ditch around all of the sashing and the Nine Patch blocks. Outline quilt around each appliqué design. Quilt a checked design in the blue center of the quilt.

3 Add a hanging sleeve if desired.

4 Use the 2½"-wide green dot strips to make the binding. Sew the binding to the quilt. Add a label if desired.

Tennis Star Pillow

Made by DeElda Wittmack. Quilted by Margaret Sindelar.

This special tennis-theme pillow has a more feminine look to recognize an outstanding athletic achievement by your favorite young lady. What daughter, granddaughter, niece, or special friend wouldn't love to have this on her bed? The black-and-white ruffle on this pillow makes it whimsical. Remember that when enlarging a design for a pillow, the finishing touches are what make it masculine or feminine. This same tennis design with the checks used as a border instead of a ruffle would be perfect for any male tennis champ you know.

Finished Pillow: 14" x 14" with a 3" ruffle ■ Finished Block: 14" x 14"

MATERIALS

All yardages are based on 42"-wide fabric unless otherwise noted. Fat quarters measure 18" x 21".

½ yard of pink print for pillow background and backing

½ yard of lime green print for tennis balls and bias piping

½ yard of black fabric for checked ruffle

½ yard of white fabric for checked ruffle

¼ yard of dark gray print for tennis racket

⅛ yard of purple checked fabric for tennis net

1 fat quarter of yellow print for star

6" x 8" piece of light gray print for tennis racket face

⅝ yard of muslin for pillow lining

2 squares, 18" x 18", of batting for pillow

½ yard of fusible web

½ yard of stabilizer

Threads to match fabric for appliqué

2 yards of ¼"-diameter cotton cording for piping

14" x 14" pillow form

CUTTING

All measurements include ¼" seam allowances. Cut all strips across the width of the fabric (selvage to selvage).

From the pink print, cut:
2 squares, 15" x 15"

From the lime green print, cut:
2"-wide bias strips to total 72"

From the black fabric, cut:
4 strips, 3½" x 42"

From the white fabric, cut:
4 strips, 3½" x 42"

From the muslin, cut:
2 squares, 18" x 18"

From the stabilizer, cut:
1 square, 15" x 15"

APPLIQUÉING THE BLOCK

Enlarge the tennis design on page 62 to 233% to measure 14" square, and the star design on page 61 to 150% to measure 9" square. Refer to "Machine Appliqué" on page 7 to prepare and cut the appliqué shapes of the star, tennis racket, tennis racket face, and three tennis balls. Prepare the tennis net using fusible web and cut along the straight lines of fabric.

1 Pin the 15" square of stabilizer to the wrong side of a 15" pink square.

2 Using the pattern as a layout guide, fuse and appliqué the net, star, tennis racket, tennis racket face, and balls following the number sequence on the pattern. Notice that the large star replaces the sun. Use a wider satin stitch on the top edge of the net to represent the tape on a tennis net, and a shorter satin stitch along the bottom edge of the net.

3 Hand or machine embroider any wording you wish to add.

4 Gently remove the stabilizer, press, and trim the block to 14½" square.

BLACK-AND-WHITE RUFFLE

1 Sew one 3½" x 42" black strip and one 3½" x 42" white strip together to make a strip set; press. Make four strip sets. Cut the strip sets into 3½"-wide segments. Cut 44 segments.

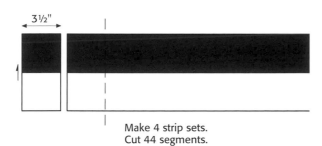

3½"

Make 4 strip sets.
Cut 44 segments.

2 Sew the segments from step 1 together, alternating the black squares and white squares as shown, to make a continuous strip that measures approximately 132". Join the two

ends of the strip to make a continuous loop. Press the seam allowances open to reduce bulk.

3 Fold the ruffle in half lengthwise, wrong sides together, and press. Using a longer stitch length, sew a gathering stitch the length of the ruffle, a scant ¼" in from the raw edge.

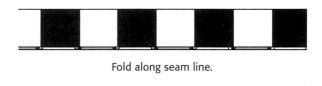

Fold along seam line.

Stitch ¼" from raw edge.

FINISHING THE PILLOW

Refer to "Finishing Your Quilt" on page 10 for details on quilt finishing if needed.

1 Layer the pillow top with 18" squares of batting and muslin. Baste the layers together.

2 Layer the 15"-square pink pillow back with 18" squares of batting and muslin. Make sure that the pillow back is centered over the batting and muslin. Baste the layers together.

3 Hand or machine quilt both the front and back of the pillow as desired. You may wish to outline quilt around each appliqué design in the pillow top. Quilt a few stars on the pillow back.

4 After quilting, trim the muslin and batting even with the pillow top. Measure through the center and trim the pillow back to that measurement.

5 Sew the lime green bias strips together to make a continuous strip. You will use this strip to cover the cording and make the piping. Refer to "Covering Cording" on page 13 as needed. Trim the seam allowance evenly to ¼".

6 Align the raw edges of the pillow top and piping. Sew the piping around the edge of the pillow top with a ¼" seam allowance. Start in the middle of the bottom edge and stitch around the pillow, overlapping the beginning and ending tails of the piping as shown. Stitch across the piping where the tails cross. Trim the ends of the piping even with the raw edge of the pillow top.

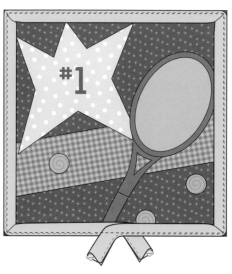

Align raw edges of piping and pillow top.
Stitch ¼" from edges.

7 Gather the ruffle, adjusting the fullness, and place it on top of the piping. Match the raw edges. Using the zipper foot, sew the ruffle to the edges of the pillow top with a ¼" seam allowance.

Align raw edges of pillow top, piping,
and ruffle. Stitch ¼" from edges.

8 With the pillow top on top, place the front and back of the pillow right sides together and sew around the edges with a ¼" seam allowance. Leave an 8" to 10" opening to turn the pillow right sides out. Backstitch along each side of the opening.

9 Turn the pillow right side out. Insert the pillow form and close the opening with a slip stitch.

VARIATION: CHECKED BORDER

Here's a more tailored version of the single-block pillow. Instead of a ruffle, add a checked border and covered cording to finish it off.

To create this pillow, enlarge a design to measure 14" and appliqué it to a background that's 15" square. Trim the completed block to 14½". Make a checked border using one 2½" x 42" strip each of black and white fabric. Referring to the directions in "Finishing the Pillow" on page 31, add covered cording using ½" diameter cording and 3"-wide bias strips. Complete the pillow and insert an 18" x 18" pillow form.

Made by DeElda Wittmack. Quilted by Margaret Sindelar.

Man's Best Friend and Toys Wall Hanging

Made by DeElda Wittmack. Quilted by Ruth Smith.

What two subjects could make a guy or gal happier than their favorite pet and most beloved sports equipment? For this whimsical hanging, I made the dog purple. Why not? I think this would make a darling headboard for the bed in a little boy's room. Start with a fun color for the dog and add the equipment of your choice.

Finished Size of Wall Hanging: 39" x 21"

MATERIALS

All yardages are based on 42"-wide fabric unless otherwise noted. Fat quarters measure 18" x 21".

2 yards of brown print for outer borders, binding, and backing

½ yard of turquoise dot print for sky

¼ yard of yellow print for inner borders

¼ yard of green print for grass

1 fat quarter of purple print for dog

6" x 6" square of white print for volleyball

6" x 10" rectangle of brown print for football

2" x 5" rectangle of white fabric for lace area of football

2" x 9" rectangle of light gold print for baseball bat

4" x 4" square of brown print for baseball mitt

2" x 2" square of cream fabric for baseball

7" x 7" square of rust print for basketball

3" x 12" rectangle of dark gold print for hockey stick

3" x 11" rectangle of gray print for lacrosse stick

3" x 4" rectangle of grayish black print for lacrosse net

6" x 6" square of white print for soccer ball

5" x 5" square of black print for soccer ball

5" x 10" rectangle of dark gray print for tennis racket

4" x 5" rectangle of light gray print for tennis racket face

Scrap of light pink print for dog's ears and nose

2 scraps—any color—for hockey stick tape

Scrap of black fabric for hockey puck

Scrap of dark orange print for lacrosse ball

Scrap of yellow print for 3 tennis balls

Scrap of white fabric for dog's eye

26" x 46" piece of batting

1 yard of fusible web

1 yard of stabilizer to cover back

6 sheets, 8½" x 11", of stabilizer

Red thread for baseball

Thread to match and contrast fabric for appliqué

Fabric paint for dog eye

CUTTING

All measurements include ¼" seam allowances. Cut all strips across the width of the fabric (selvage to selvage).

From the turquoise dot print, cut:
1 rectangle, 13½" x 34"

From the green print, cut:
1 rectangle, 3½" x 34"

From the yellow print for inner borders, cut:
4 strips, 1" x 42"

From the 2 yards of brown print, cut:
4 strips, 3" x 42"

4 strips, 2½" x 42"

From the yard of stabilizer, cut:
1 piece, 17" x 34"

MAN'S BEST FRIEND AND TOYS WALL HANGING

ASSEMBLING THE WALL HANGING

Refer to "Machine Appliqué" on page 7 to prepare and cut the appliqué shapes as listed in the materials section.

1 Sew the 13½" x 34" turquoise dot print rectangle to the long side of the 3½" x 34" green print rectangle. Press the seam allowance open. Pin a 17" x 34" piece of stabilizer to the back and set it aside until step 11.

2 Pin an 8½" x 11" piece of stabilizer under the dog and each piece of sports equipment that requires stitching detail.

3 Paint the dog's eye and let it dry. Refer to "Painting on Fabric" on page 6 as needed. Cut out and appliqué the painted eye onto the dog shape. Appliqué the ears and nose.

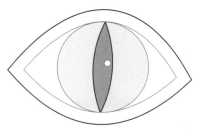

Dog eye pattern including ⅛" seam allowance

4 Appliqué each black pentagon shape to the white soccer ball.

5 Appliqué the racket face to the tennis racket.

6 Appliqué the tape sections to the hockey stick.

7 Appliqué the lace area to the football.

8 Appliqué the basket netting to the lacrosse stick.

9 Refer to each pattern and the photo on page 23 to sew all the details in each appliqué shape using a satin stitch. Don't sew around the outside edge.

10 Remove the stabilizer and the fusible web paper so that the fusible web will adhere to the background.

11 Without fusing, position the dog in the middle of the unit from step 1 and arrange the sports

equipment in a pleasing display around the dog. Refer to the photo on page 23. You may wish to fuse one shape at a time so that you can make small changes if needed.

⓬ Fuse and appliqué the shapes to the background in the order listed in "D's Tip" on page 25, checking placement as you work. Several of the pieces will sit on the grass, but a few will come down over the grass area to make a more pleasing design. Some shapes are in front of others, so work slowly and refer to the photo on page 23 as needed. Note that you should place the baseball in the dog's mouth before fusing the dog in place.

⓭ Gently remove the stabilizer. Press and trim the wall hanging to 15½" x 33½".

ADDING THE BORDERS

For detailed instructions, refer to "Adding Borders" on page 10.

❶ Measure the quilt through the center from side to side and trim two 1"-wide yellow inner-border strips to fit that measurement.

❷ Sew the trimmed border strips to the top and bottom edges of the quilt top. Press toward the border strip.

❸ Measure the quilt through the center from top to bottom, including the borders just added. Trim the remaining 1"-wide yellow inner-border strips to fit that measurement.

❹ Sew the trimmed border strips to the side edges of the quilt top; press.

❺ Repeat steps 1–4 to measure, trim, and add the 3"-wide brown outer-border strips. Press toward the outer-border strips.

FINISHING THE QUILT

Refer to "Finishing Your Quilt" on page 10 for details on quilt finishing if needed.

❶ Cut and piece, if needed, the brown backing fabric so that it is approximately 4" to 6" larger than the quilt top. Layer the quilt top with batting and backing. Baste the layers together.

❷ Hand or machine quilt as desired. You may wish to quilt in the ditch around the borders. Outline quilt around each appliqué shape and quilt clouds in the turquoise sky.

❸ Add a hanging sleeve if desired.

❹ Use the 2½"-wide brown strips to make the binding. Sew the binding to the quilt. Add a label if desired.

Quilt assembly

MAN'S BEST FRIEND AND TOYS WALL HANGING

Four-Square Floor Pillow

Designed by DeElda Wittmack. Made and quilted by Margaret Sindelar.

A family with sports interests needs a large floor pillow on which to lounge while watching sports events on television. This is the pattern for just such a project. Choose four designs and get to work. While the sports enthusiasts are tuned to the tube, you can be making a pillow that will get plenty of compliments plus lots of use by your family. The interesting and fun part of making this oversized pillow is the rotation of the design squares. One side of the pillow is always right side up!

Finished Pillow: 31" x 31" ■ Finished Block: 9" x 9"

MATERIALS

All yardages are based on 42"-wide fabric unless otherwise noted. Fabrics that are used in more than one block are listed below. Fabrics needed for one block only are listed in the individual block materials lists that follow.

1¾ yards of medium-weight blue denim for piping and pillow backing

⅔ yard of blue floral print for sashing and borders

¼ yard of black fabric for checkerboard border

¼ yard of white fabric for checkerboard border

⅜ yard of grass green print for backgrounds in Football, Baseball, and Soccer blocks

⅜ yard of light green print for background in Hockey block and diamond in Baseball block

⅓ yard of light blue print for sky in Football and Soccer blocks

¼ yard of white print for football laces, top of hockey skate blade, and soccer ball

1⅛ yards of muslin for pillow lining

35" x 35" piece of batting

1 yard of fusible web

4 sheets, 8½" x 11" (or 1⅜ yards), of stabilizer

Thread to match and contrast fabric for appliqué

3¾ yards of ½"-diameter cotton cording

32" x 32" pillow form

Football Block

6" x 10" rectangle of rust fabric for football

4" x 4" square of orange print for sunbeams

2" x 2" square of yellow print for sun

Baseball Block

2" x 9" rectangle of beige print for baseball bat

4" x 4" square of brown print for baseball mitt

4 squares, 2" x 2", of gray print for bases and home plate

2" x 2" square of off-white print for baseball

Hockey Block

6" x 8" rectangle of black print for skate

4" x 12" rectangle of brown print for hockey stick

1" x 8" rectangle of turquoise print for base of skate boot

2" x 8" rectangle of gray print for skate blade

2" x 2" square of black dot print for hockey puck

Scraps of orange for hockey stick

Fabric paint (or eyelet kit) for skate eyelets

Soccer Block

⅛ yard of black print for soccer ball

CUTTING

All measurements include ¼" seam allowances. Cut all strips across the width of the fabric (selvage to selvage).

From the grass green print, cut:
2 rectangles, 4¼" x 11"
1 square, 11" x 11"

From the light blue print, cut:
2 rectangles, 7¼" x 11"

From the light green print, cut:
1 square, 11" x 11"
1 square, 6" x 6"

From the black fabric, cut:
4 strips, 1½" x 42"

From the white fabric, cut:
4 strips, 1½" x 42"

From the blue floral print, cut:
2 strips, 3½" x 31½"
2 strips, 3½" x 25½"
2 strips, 3½" x 42"; cut into 4 rectangles, 3½" x 11½"
1 square, 1½" x 1½"

From the blue denim, cut:
1 square, 33" x 33"
3"-wide bias strips to total 135"

From the muslin, cut:
1 square, 35" x 35"

From the stabilizer, cut:
4 squares, 11" x 11"

APPLIQUÉING THE BLOCKS

Enlarge the block patterns for this project (pages 45–63) 150% to measure 9" square. Refer to "Machine Appliqué" on page 7 to prepare and cut the appliqué shapes as listed in the materials section.

Pin a square of stabilizer to the back of each block before starting to appliqué. Appliqué the shapes in the number sequence on each block pattern. Using the pattern as a layout guide, fuse each shape and appliqué around it. Refer to each pattern and the photo on page 27 for the individual stitch details within each block. The following block instructions provide additional construction and detailing information.

Football Block

1. Sew a 4¼" x 11" grass green rectangle and a 7¼" x 11" light blue rectangle together to make the block background. Press toward the green fabric.

2. After stitching around each shape, use a dark gray thread and a satin stitch to sew a line through the football center. Add crosshatch lines for the lacing.

Baseball Block

When stitching the mitt, use a satin stitch to add the webbing and finger details. Before appliquéing around the baseball, stitch the red seams on the ball using a satin stitch.

Hockey Block

Note that the hockey stick is cut as one piece. The orange strips are fused onto the stick and trimmed before fusing the stick to the background. The boot is also cut as one piece. Stitch the detail on the boot using a grey thread and a satin stitch. Paint the eyelets or add real eyelets following the directions on an eyelet kit.

Soccer Block

Note that you should cut the white soccer ball as one piece, and then appliqué each black pentagon shape to complete the ball.

1. Sew a 4¼" x 11" grass green rectangle and a 7¼" x 11" light blue rectangle together to make the block background. Press toward the green fabric.

2. After appliquéing the ball to the background, mark the additional section lines on the ball with a quilter's permanent pen. Stitch on the drawn lines using a satin stitch and black thread.

FINISHING THE BLOCKS

1. Gently remove the stabilizer from the blocks. Press and trim all four completed blocks to measure 9½" square.

2. Sew the 1½"-wide black and white strips into four strip sets as shown. Press toward the black strip.

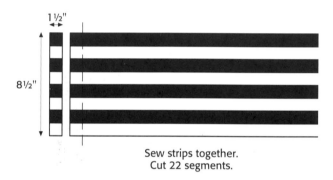

Make 4 strip sets.

3. Alternate and sew the four strip sets from step 2 together as shown to make a strip set measuring 8½" wide. Crosscut the strip set into 22 segments, 1½" wide.

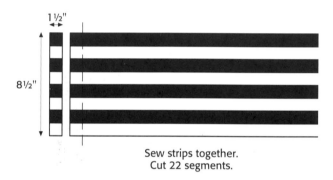

Sew strips together.
Cut 22 segments.

4. Sew the segments together end to end to make a long strip, alternating the black squares and white squares as shown; press.

5. Using a seam ripper, gently remove lines of stitches to separate the long strip from step 4 into smaller strips. You'll need eight strips, each measuring 9½" long and beginning and ending with a white square, and eight strips, each measuring 11½" long and beginning and ending with a black square.

9½"

Make 8.

11½"

Make 8.

6. Sew a 9½" strip to the top and bottom edges of each appliqué block. Press toward the block center. Sew an 11½" strip to each of the side edges as shown; press. The blocks should measure 11½" square.

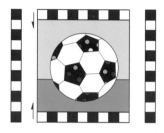

ASSEMBLING THE PILLOW TOP

1. From the remaining strip of black-and-white squares, separate the seams to make two 3½"-long strips with a black square on each end, and two 1½" white squares.

2. Sew the 1½" blue floral square between the two 1½" white squares from step 1. Press toward the blue square.

3. Sew the unit from step 2 between the two black-and-white strips from step 1 to make a Nine Patch block as shown; press.

4. Arrange the appliqué blocks, the Nine Patch block from step 3, and four 3½" x 11½" blue rectangles, making sure to rotate the appliqué blocks as shown. Sew the blocks and rectangles in rows; press. Sew the rows together; press.

FOUR-SQUARE FLOOR PILLOW

⑤ Sew the 3½" x 25½" blue floral strips to the side edges of the pillow top; press. Sew the 3½" x 31½" strips to the top and bottom edges; press.

FINISHING THE PILLOW

Refer to "Finishing Your Quilt" on page 10 for details on quilt finishing if needed.

① Layer the pillow top with batting and muslin. Baste the layers together.

② Hand or machine quilt the pillow top as desired. You may wish to quilt the pillow top in the ditch on both sides of the black-and-white checks and outline quilt around each appliqué design. The denim backing fabric on the pillow back is heavy enough to not need quilting unless desired.

③ After quilting, trim the backing and batting even with the pillow top. Measure through the center and trim the pillow back to that measurement.

④ Sew the denim bias strips together to make a continuous strip. You will use this strip to cover the cording and make the piping. Refer to "Covering Cording" on page 13 as needed. Trim the seam allowance evenly to ¼".

⑤ Align the raw edges of the pillow top and piping. Using a zipper foot, sew the piping around the edge of the pillow top with a ¼" seam allowance. Start in the middle of the bottom edge and stitch around the pillow. Stop sewing approximately 6" away from the starting point. Cut the piping so that the two tails overlap 1". Open the stitches on one tail and cut off 1" of just the cording, not the fabric covering. Turn the cut edge of the fabric under ¼" as shown, insert the beginning tail, refold the fabric to cover all raw edges, and continue the seam.

Align raw edges of pillow front and piping.
Stitch ¼" from edges.

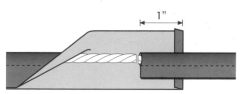

⑥ With the pillow top on top, place the front and back of the pillow right sides together and sew around the edges. Leave an 18" to 22" opening to turn the pillow right sides out. Backstitch along each side of the opening.

⑦ Clip the corners and turn the pillow right side out. Insert the pillow form and close the opening with a slip stitch.

Rocky Mountain High
Wall Hanging

Made by DeElda Wittmack. Quilted by Ruth Smith.

This vertical quilted wall hanging incorporates three different sports and some beautiful purple mountains. Mountain biking, skiing, and fly-fishing are sports that many enjoy when vacationing in the mountains.

Three appliqué blocks are used to make this wall hanging. The enlarged skis were extracted from the skiing design and appliquéd to the outer borders. Since the skis are appliquéd over the border fabric, you can simply omit them if skiing isn't one of your favorite sports.

Any of the appliqué blocks could be used in this vertical design. If you're not fond of winter and snow, choose a floral for the border to remind you of summer wildflowers. Turn the mountain bike into a road bike by substituting a gray pavement print for the brown print. Add a block with a motorboat or sailboat, and a block with a golf theme, and you have the perfect way to remember a favorite summer vacation.

Finished Wall Hanging: 15" x 32" ■ Finished Individual Blocks: 8" x 8"

MATERIALS

All yardages are based on 42"-wide fabric unless otherwise noted. Fabrics that are used in more than one block and the borders are listed below. Fabrics needed for one block only are listed in the individual block materials lists that follow.

1¼ yards of blue snowflake print for borders, backing, and binding

⅓ yard of turquoise dot print for sky in blocks

¼ yard of black solid for checked sashing

¼ yard of white fabric for checked sashing

¼ yard of red print for tops of skis

¼ yard of black print for bottoms of skis

⅛ yard of gray print for ski poles

4" x 6" piece of green print for pole straps

19" x 36" piece of batting

1 yard of fusible web

1⅜ yards of stabilizer

Thread to match and contrast fabric for appliqué

Skiing Block

4" x 9" rectangle of dark green print for grass

3" x 9" rectangle of purple print for mountains

3" x 9" rectangle of white print for mountain snow

2" x 2" square of yellow print for sun

Fishing Block

4" x 7" rectangle of blue print for water

4" x 7" rectangle of rainbow fabric for trout

1" x 2" rectangle of dark gray print for fishing pole handle

2" x 2" square of gray for fishing reel

Small scrap of red-and-white stripe for bobber

Small scrap of fabric printed with fishing flies, or a small colorful feather for lure

Biking Block

4" x 9" rectangle of brown print for dirt

4" x 8" rectangle of black print for bike tires

4" x 7" rectangle of red print for bike frame

Scrap of green print for bike seat

CUTTING

All measurements include ¼" seam allowances. Cut all strips across the width of the fabric (selvage to selvage).

From the turquoise dot print, cut

2 rectangles, 6" x 9"

1 square, 9" x 9"

From the black solid, cut:

2 strips, 1½" x 15"

From the white fabric, cut:

2 strips, 1½" x 15"

From the blue snowflake print, cut:

2 strips, 4" x 42"

3 strips, 2½" x 42"

2 rectangles, 3" x 8½"

From the stabilizer, cut:

3 squares, 9" x 9"

2 pieces, 4" x 28"

APPLIQUÉING THE BLOCKS

Enlarge the block patterns for this project (pages 45–63) 133% to measure 8" square. Refer to "Machine Appliqué" on page 7 to prepare and cut the appliqué shapes as listed in the materials section.

Pin a square of stabilizer to the back of each block before starting to appliqué. Appliqué the shapes in the number sequence on each block pattern. Refer to each pattern and the photo on page 32 for the individual stitch details within each block. The following block instructions provide additional construction and detailing information.

Skiing Block

1. Sew a 6" x 9" turquoise rectangle and a 4" x 9" dark green rectangle together to make the block background. Press the seam allowance open.

2. Using the pattern as a layout guide, fuse each shape and appliqué around it. Appliqué the bottom edge of the mountains first, and then add the snow. Appliqué both the top and bottom edges of the snow and finish with the sun.

Fishing Block

D'S TIP

Draw and cut a circle proportional to the size of the red-and-white stripe fabric. After preparing the stripe fabric with fusible web, place the circle on the stripe as shown and cut out the circle to make the fishing bobber.

Cut a circle proportional to the stripes.

1. Using the pattern as a layout guide, fuse each shape to the 9" x 9" turquoise square and appliqué around the shape. After appliquéing the fish, add the fin details, and paint or appliqué the eye.

2. Using a quilter's permanent pen, draw a straight line from the fishing pole handle upward to make the fishing rod. Draw the ferrules and tippet (the little eyelets on the rod and at the end that hold the fishing line), and the handle of the fishing reel. Stitch on the drawn lines using a medium-width satin stitch and gray thread.

3. Using the pattern as a guide, draw the fishing line with a water-soluble marker. Use a very small straight stitch to sew the fishing line. Be sure to stop and start on each side of the bobber.

4. Fussy cut a small fishing fly from the fishing-fly fabric and tack it with several hand stitches to the mouth of the fish. Or cut a small piece of feather and tack it to the fish mouth.

Biking Block

1. Sew a 6" x 9" turquoise rectangle and a 4" x 9" brown print rectangle together to make the block background. Press the seam allowance open.

2. Using the pattern as a layout guide, fuse each shape and appliqué around it. Use a dark gray thread and satin stitch to make the bike pedal.

ASSEMBLING THE QUILT TOP

1. Gently remove the stabilizer from the blocks. Press and trim all three completed blocks to measure 8½" square.

2. Sew the 1½"-wide black and white strips into two strip sets as shown. Press toward the black strip.

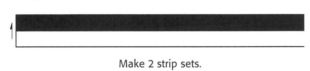

Make 2 strip sets.

3. Alternate and sew the two strip sets from step 2 together as shown to make a strip set measuring 4½" wide. Crosscut the strip set into seven segments, 1½" wide.

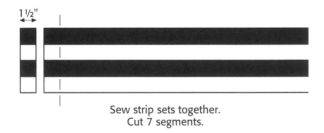

Sew strip sets together.
Cut 7 segments.

4. Sew the segments together end to end to make a long strip, alternating the black squares and white squares as shown; press.

5. Using a seam ripper, gently remove lines of stitches to separate the long strip from step 4 into three strips, each measuring 9½" long and beginning and ending with a white square.

6. Center and sew a 9½" strip of checks to the bottom edge of each appliqué block. Then trim the excess white fabric even with the edges of the block. Press toward the block.

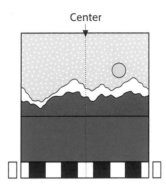

Trim excess white fabric.

7. Sew the three blocks together in a vertical row.

ADDING THE BORDERS

For detailed instructions, refer to "Adding Borders" on page 10.

1. Sew the 3" x 8½" blue snowflake rectangles to the top and bottom edges. Press toward the borders.

2. Measure the quilt through the center from top to bottom, and trim two 4"-wide blue snowflake border strips to fit that measurement.

3. Sew the trimmed border strips to the side edges of the quilt top. Press toward the border strip.

4. Using the pattern below and on page 37, and a large sheet of paper, trace the top parts of both the skis and poles. Extend the drawing down for 17", and then add the bottoms of the skis and poles. The total length of the skis should be 28". The poles measure 23½" from the top of the pole strap to the pole point.

5. Refer to the photo on page 32 and "Machine Appliqué" on page 7 to prepare and cut your ski and pole shapes for appliqué. Fuse the skis next to the block and border seam line, pin the 4" x 28" pieces of stabilizer to the back, and appliqué around the skis and pole shapes. Be sure to notice that the pole strap wraps around and under the ski tip. Position the red ski top slightly over the black ski bottom. Appliqué the outer edge of the black ski bottoms and both sides of the red ski tops. Gently remove the stabilizer and press.

FINISHING THE QUILT

Refer to "Finishing Your Quilt" on page 10 for details on quilt finishing if needed.

1. If needed, cut and piece the backing fabric so that it is approximately 4" to 6" larger than the quilt top. Layer the quilt top with batting and backing. Baste the layers together.

2. Hand or machine quilt as desired. You may wish to quilt in the ditch along the seam lines and on both sides of the checked strips. Outline quilt around each appliqué design, as well as the skis and poles.

3. Use the 2½"-wide blue snowflake strips to make the binding. Sew the binding to the quilt. Add a label if desired.

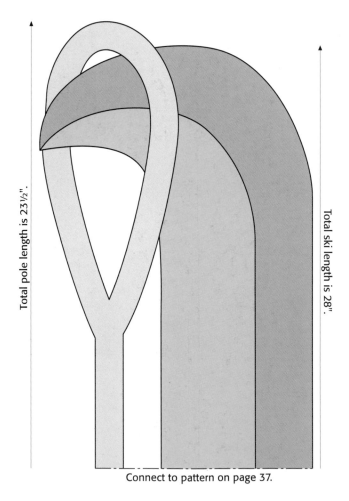

Total pole length is 23½".

Total ski length is 28".

Connect to pattern on page 37.

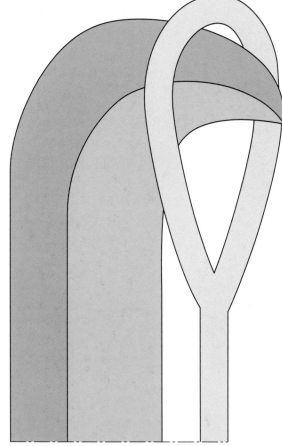

Connect to pattern on page 37.

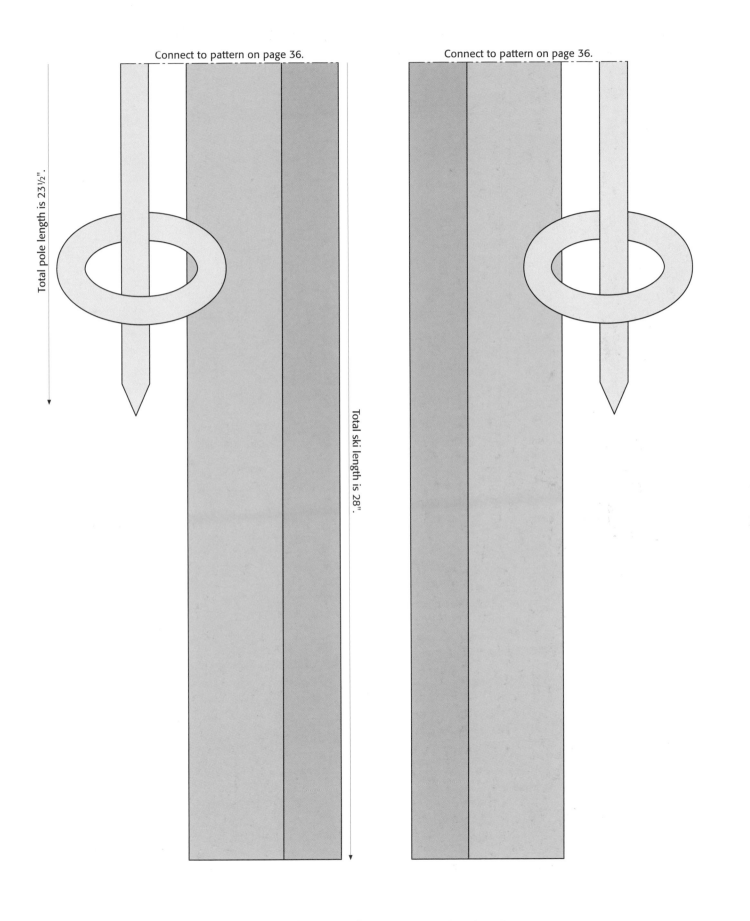

Connect to pattern on page 36.

Connect to pattern on page 36.

Total pole length is 23½".

Total ski length is 28".

ROCKY MOUNTAIN HIGH WALL HANGING

Sports Galore Quilt

Made by DeElda Wittmack and Ruth Smith. Quilted by Donna Horn.

This is the perfect project for the hard-to-buy-for sports fanatic on your holiday or birthday list. Remember, you're the designer, so change designs around, incorporate your favorite team colors into the finished quilt, and play with the appliqué.

Finished Quilt Size: 52" x 74" ■ Finished Block Size: 9" x 9"

MATERIALS

All yardages are based on 42"-wide fabric unless otherwise noted. Fabrics that are used in more than one block and the borders are listed below. Fabrics needed for one block only are listed in the individual block instructions starting on page 40.

4 yards of dark purple dot print for backing and binding

2 yards of dark turquoise print for outer border

1¾ yards of purple print for sashing strips and inner borders

⅜ yard of black fabric for checked border

⅜ yard of white fabric for checked border

⅜ yard of medium green print for Golf, Tennis, Soccer, Lacrosse, Baseball, and Canoe blocks

⅜ yard of turquoise sky print for Sailboat, Tennis, Biking, and Soccer blocks

⅜ yard of blue dot sky print for Fishing, Football, Canoe, and Skiing blocks

⅜ yard of blue cloud sky print for Golf, Motorboat, and Lacrosse blocks

⅜ yard of yellow print for Volleyball, Basketball, and Hockey blocks

⅜ yard of blue water print for Sailboat, Fishing, Canoe, and Motorboat blocks

¼ yard of lime green print for Golf, Baseball, Football, and Canoe blocks

¼ yard of dark green print for Skiing and Canoe blocks

Scraps of 3 to 4 yellow prints for suns

6 squares, 4" x 4", of various oranges for sunrays

56" x 78" piece of batting

3½ yards of fusible web (you may have some left over)

15 sheets, 8½" x 11", of stabilizer

Thread to match and contrast fabric for appliqué

D'S TIP

When picking fabrics for this large quilt, select two or three that you can use several times. I picked a blue fabric that I used for all the water appliqué pieces. Two to three blue or turquoise fabrics for sky can be enough for a quilt of this size. Do the same with green fabrics, being careful to vary the use of each around the quilt. When picking a background color for the blocks without a sky, remember to pick one that balances with or complements the other blocks. I often use yellow—not because I love yellow but because I feel it brings light to the project and picks up the other colors. Scatter these "skyless" blocks across the quilt because the strong color will draw your eye around the project.

CUTTING

All measurements include ¼" seam allowances. Cut all strips across the width of the fabric (selvage to selvage). Cutting instructions for the fabrics that are used in the blocks are listed in the individual block instructions starting in "Appliquéing the Blocks" below.

From the lengthwise grain of the purple print fabric, cut:
2 strips, 3¼" x 63"
2 strips, 2½" x 43"
4 strips, 3¼" x 33"
10 strips, 3¼" x 9½"

From the black fabric, cut:
4 strips, 2½" x 42"

From the white fabric, cut:
4 strips, 2½" x 42"

From the lengthwise grain of the dark turquoise print, cut:
4 strips, 5½" x 72"

From the dark purple dot print, cut:
7 strips, 2½" x 42"

APPLIQUÉING THE BLOCKS

Enlarge the block patterns for this project (pages 45–63) 150% to measure 9" square. Refer to "Machine Appliqué" on page 7 to prepare and cut the appliqué shapes as listed in the materials section and under the individual block instructions that follow.

Pin a square of stabilizer to the back of each block before starting the appliqué. Refer to each pattern and the photo on page 38 as a layout guide. Then fuse each shape and appliqué around it in the number sequence on each pattern. Next, sew the individual stitch details within each block. Additional fabric and cutting requirements, block directions, and detailing information are listed in the individual block instructions that follow.

D'S TIP

Fuse the appliqué shapes on all of the blocks before starting to appliqué. This enables you to work on several blocks at one time and reduces the number of times you have to change thread colors on your sewing machine.

Baseball Block

5" x 5" square of rust print for baseball mitt

2" x 9" rectangle of brown wood print for bat

2" x 4" rectangle of gray print for bases

2" x 2" square of cream print for baseball

Cut an 11" square from the medium green print (see "Materials" on page 39) for the outfield background. Use the lime green print (see "Materials") to cut and fuse the infield. After appliquéing the ball, use red thread and a satin stitch to stitch the seams on the ball.

Basketball Block

8" x 8" square of brown print for basketball

5" x 5" square of white print for backboard

3" x 3" square of checked fabric for net

Cut an 11" square from the yellow print (see "Materials" on page 39) for the background. If desired, draw the lines in the net area with a quilter's permanent pen. Using a straight or satin stitch, follow the lines to stitch the basketball net.

Biking Block

4" x 8" rectangle of black print for tires

2½" x 11" rectangle of gray print for road

5" x 6" rectangle of red print for bike frame

Scrap of turquoise print for bike seat

Cut an 8½" x 11" rectangle from the turquoise sky print (see "Materials" on page 39). Sew the sky and road rectangles together to make the block background; press the seam allowance open. Use a dark thread and a satin stitch to make the bike pedal.

Canoeing Block

3" x 10" rectangle of gray print for canoe

½" x 10" rectangle of red print for canoe trim

2" x 7" rectangle of brown print for paddle

Scrap of white for moon

Cut a 6" x 11" rectangle from the blue dot sky print and a 5" x 11" rectangle from the blue water print (see "Materials" on page 39). Sew the sky and water rectangles together to make the block background; press the seam allowance open. Use the medium green print, lime green print, and dark green print (see "Materials") to cut and fuse the trees. Remember to overlap them so that they will look like a real forest. The canoe can also be straightened in the water if you prefer.

Fishing Block

4" x 8" rectangle of rainbow print for fish

Scrap of black print for fishing pole handle

Scrap of gray print for fishing reel

Small scrap of red-and-white stripe for bobber

Small scrap of fabric printed with fishing flies, or small colorful feather for lure

Cut an 11" square from the blue dot sky print for the block background and use the blue water print for the water (see "Materials" on page 39). After appliquéing the fish, add the fin details. Then paint or appliqué the eye, adding a white dot for a realistic look. Appliqué the fishing pole handle and reel. Then use a quilter's permanent pen to draw a straight line from the handle upward to make the fishing rod. Add the notches for the rod eyelets and the handle on the reel. Stitch on the lines using a medium-width satin stitch and gray thread.

Refer to "D's Tip" on page 34 to make the bobber; appliqué it in place. With a water-soluble marker, draw the fishing line as shown on the pattern. Use black thread and sew the line with a very short straight stitch. Fussy cut a lure from fabric and tack it with several stitches to the mouth of the fish, or sew a small piece of feather to the fish's mouth to resemble a lure.

Football Block

6" x 10" rectangle of brown print for football

2" x 5" rectangle of cream print for lace area of football

Cut a 7" x 11" rectangle from the blue dot sky print and a 4" x 11" rectangle from the lime green print (see "Materials" on page 39). Sew the rectangles together to make the block background. Press the seam allowance open.

After appliquéing the football and lace area, use a quilter's permanent pen to draw a straight line on the football from point to point. Sew a small satin stitch over the line. Then mark and stitch the laces using a dark gray thread.

Golfing Block

2" x 4" rectangle of red dot print for flag

2" x 4" rectangle of tan print for sand trap

2" x 2" square of off-white print for golf ball

1" x 3" rectangle of purple print for golf tee

Scrap of cream for golf hole

Scrap of brown print for wood head

Scrap of gray for iron heads

Scrap of charcoal or black print for club handles

Cut a 6" x 11" rectangle from the blue cloud sky print and a 6" x 11" rectangle from the medium green print (see "Materials" on page 39). Appliqué the sun and sunrays to the sky; then stitch the sky and green rectangles together. The bottom edges of the appliqué pieces will be sewn into the seam allowance. Press toward the green.

After appliquéing the golf hole, use a quilter's permanent pen to draw a straight line for the flagpole; use the pattern as a guide. Appliqué the flag. Use a wide satin stitch and dark gray thread to sew the flagpole, covering the drawn line and catching the edge of the flag.

Appliqué each of the golf club heads. Repeat the process above to draw lines for the club shafts from the heads to where the handles will be. Then, using a light gray thread, sew a narrow satin stitch over the drawn lines to make the shafts. Notice that the putter shaft curves near the head. Then appliqué the handles of the three clubs over the shafts.

Stitch a little shadow of grass under the golf tee and the number of your favorite hole to the flag.

Hockey Block

6" x 8" rectangle of black print for skate

4" x 12" rectangle of brown wood print for hockey stick

2" x 8" rectangle of white print for area above skate blade

2" x 8" rectangle of gray print for skate blade

1" x 8" rectangle of purple print for base of skate boot

2" x 2" square of black dot print for hockey puck

Scraps of any color for stick wraps

Cut an 11" square from the yellow print (see "Materials" on page 39) for the block background. Note that the boot is cut from one piece of fabric. After appliquéing the boot, add the details using a light gray thread. To make the eyelets of the boot, I used the cover end of a quilter's permanent pen dipped in light gray fabric paint. The eraser end of a pencil would give a more solid eyelet.

Lacrosse Block

3" x 11" rectangle of purple print for stick

3" x 4" rectangle of black-and-white print for net

2" x 2" square of yellow print for ball

Cut a 7" x 11" rectangle from the blue cloud sky print and a 4" x 11" rectangle from the medium green print (see "Materials" on page 39). Sew the rectangles together to make the block background. Press the seam allowance open.

I was lucky enough to find a fabric that really resembled netting on a lacrosse stick. If you can't find something you like, use black netting, or simply draw a net pattern on a piece of white fabric with a quilter's permanent pen.

Motorboat Block

3" x 8" rectangle of red or rainbow print for boat hull

2" x 6" rectangle of white print for top of boat

Scrap of dark red print for seat

Scrap of gray fabric for motor

Scrap of white print for motor-fume cloud

Cut a 7" x 11" rectangle from the blue cloud sky print and use the blue water print for the water (see "Materials" on page 39). Cut the white boat top as one piece and appliqué the seat cushion over the white. After appliquéing the shapes, use the pattern as a guide to draw the boat and railing lines with a quilter's permanent pen. Sew a gray satin stitch over the lines.

Sailboat Block

5" x 6" rectangle of yellow dot print for sail

4" x 6" rectangle of green stripe print for spinnaker sail

2" x 7" rectangle of gray print for mast and boom

2" x 7" rectangle of red fabric for boat hull

1" x 3" rectangle of orange print for flag

Cut an 8" x 11" rectangle from the turquoise sky print and use the blue water print for the water (see "Materials" on page 39). After completing the appliqué, use gray thread and a satin stitch to add the line details from the sails to the boat hull.

Skiing Block

3" x 11" rectangle of purple print for mountains

3" x 11" rectangle of white print for snow

2" x 9" rectangle of black print for skis

2" x 9" rectangle of red print for ski tops

Cut a 6" x 11" rectangle from the blue dot sky print and a 5" x 11" rectangle from the dark green print (see "Materials" on page 39). Sew the rectangles together to make the block background. Press the seam allowance open. After completing the appliqué, use a quilter's permanent pen and the pattern as a guide to draw the ski poles. Sew over the drawn lines with a narrow satin stitch and gray thread to make the ski poles; the ski-pole baskets are sewn last.

Soccer Block

8" x 8" square of white print for ball

6" x 7" rectangle of black print for ball

Cut a 7" x 11" rectangle from the turquoise sky print and a 4" x 11" rectangle from the medium green print (see "Materials" on page 39). Sew the rectangles together to make the block background. Press the seam allowance open. Cut the white soccer ball as one piece, and then appliqué each black pentagon shape to complete the ball.

After appliquéing the ball to the background, mark the additional section lines on the ball with a quilter's permanent pen. Stitch on the drawn lines using a satin stitch and dark gray thread.

Tennis Block

5" x 10" rectangle of blue print for racket

4" x 11" rectangle of checked fabric for net

4" x 6" rectangle of light blue checked fabric for racket face

2" x 4" rectangle of lime print for tennis balls

1" x 2" rectangle of red print for racket handle

Cut a 7" x 11" rectangle from the turquoise sky print and a 4" x 11" rectangle from the medium green print (see "Materials" on page 39). Sew the rectangles together to make the block background. Press the seam allowance open.

A tiny checked fabric in any color would work for the racket face. Use a wider satin stitch on the top edge of the net to represent the tape on a tennis net, and a narrower satin stitch along the bottom edge of the net.

Volleyball Block

8" x 8" square of white print for volleyball

4" x 11" rectangle of light blue checked fabric for net

Cut an 11" square from the yellow print for the block background (see "Materials" on page 39). Cut the net fabric in two pieces; leave a scant seam allowance behind the volleyball to avoid the net fabric showing through the white ball.

ASSEMBLING THE QUILT TOP

1 Gently remove the stabilizer from the blocks. Press and trim all of the completed appliqué blocks to measure 9½" square.

2 Arrange and sew three appliqué blocks and two 3¼" x 9½" purple sashing strips, alternating them as shown to make a block row; press. Make five rows.

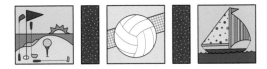

Make 5 rows.

3 Sew the 3¼" x 33" purple sashing strips between the rows. Press toward the sashing strips.

MAKING THE CHECKED BORDER

1. Sew the 2½"-wide black and white strips into four strip sets as shown. Press toward the black strip.

Make 4 strip sets.

2. Alternate and sew the four strip sets from step 1 together as shown to make a strip set measuring 16½" wide. Crosscut the strip set into 14 segments, 2½" wide.

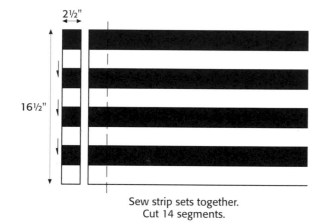

Sew strip sets together.
Cut 14 segments.

3. Sew the segments from step 2 together end to end to make a long strip, alternating the black squares and white squares; press.

4. Using a seam ripper, gently remove lines of stitches to separate the long strip from step 3 into four strips. Two strips will each be a total of 30 squares, beginning with a white square and ending with a black square. The other two strips will each be a total of 21 squares; one strip will begin and end with black squares, and the other will begin and end with white squares.

ADDING THE BORDERS

For detailed instructions, refer to "Adding Borders" on page 10. Note that for the black-and-white checked border to fit, the purple inner borders must be two different widths as noted in the cutting instructions.

1. Measure the quilt through the center from top to bottom and trim the two 3¼" x 63" purple inner-border strips to fit that measurement.

2. Sew the trimmed border strips to the side edges of the quilt top. Press toward the border strip.

3. Measure the quilt through the center from side to side, including the borders just added. It should measure 38½". Trim the 2½"-wide purple border strips to fit that measurement.

4. Sew the trimmed border strips to the top and bottom edges of the quilt top; press. The quilt top should measure 38½" x 60½" for the checked border to fit.

5. Sew the long strips from step 4 in "Making the Checked Border" to each of the side edges; press. Sew the remaining strips to the top and bottom edges, carefully matching the corners; press. Refer to the finished quilt on page 38.

6. Measure the quilt through the center as you did in steps 1–4 to add the dark turquoise 5½"-wide outer-border strips. Press toward the outer border.

FINISHING THE QUILT

Refer to "Finishing Your Quilt" on page 10 for details on quilt finishing if needed.

1. Cut and piece, if needed, the backing fabric so that it is approximately 4" to 6" larger than the quilt top. Layer the quilt top with batting and backing. Baste the layers together.

2. Hand or machine quilt as desired. You may wish to quilt in the ditch around each block and on both sides of the checked border. Outline quilt around each appliqué shape and quilt curvy, meandering lines in the sky and grass areas. Quilt a continuous design in the outer border.

3. Add a hanging sleeve if desired.

4. Use the 2½"-wide dark purple dot print strips to make the binding. Sew the binding to the quilt. Add a label if desired.

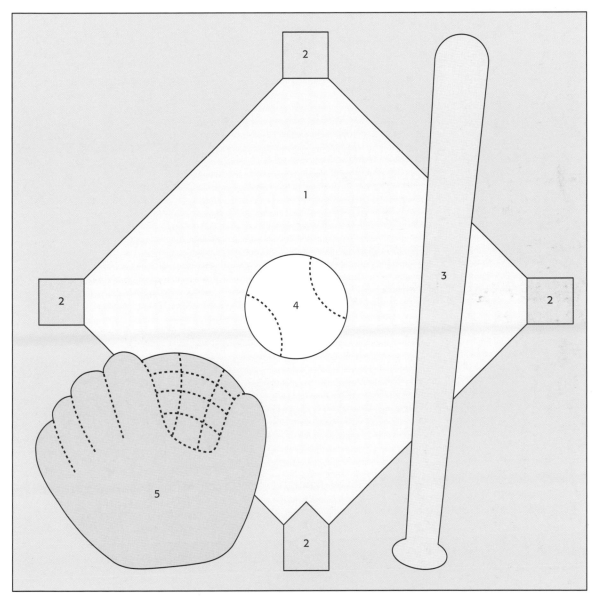

Baseball
Enlarge patterns as directed in the project instructions.
Patterns are reversed and do not include seam allowances.

- - - Satin stitch

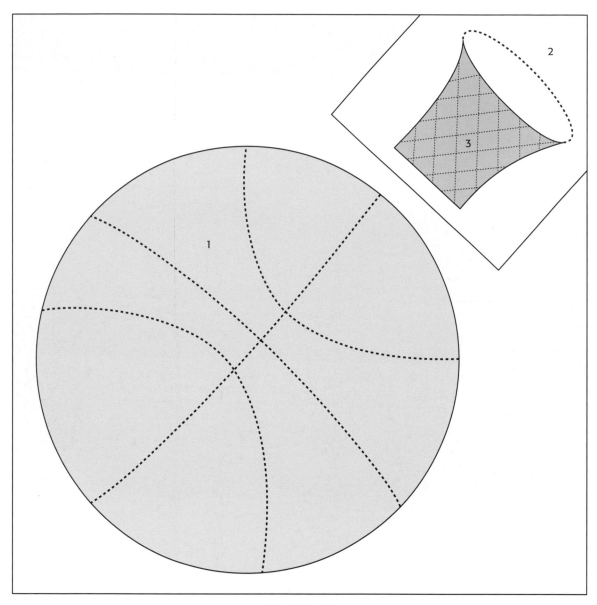

Basketball
Enlarge patterns as directed in the project instructions.
Patterns are reversed and do not include seam allowances.

- - - Satin stitch
······ Straight stitch

APPLIQUÉ DESIGNS

Biking
Enlarge patterns as directed in the project instructions.
Patterns are reversed and do not include seam allowances.

- - - Satin stitch

Canoeing
Enlarge patterns as directed in the project instructions.
Patterns are reversed and do not include seam allowances.

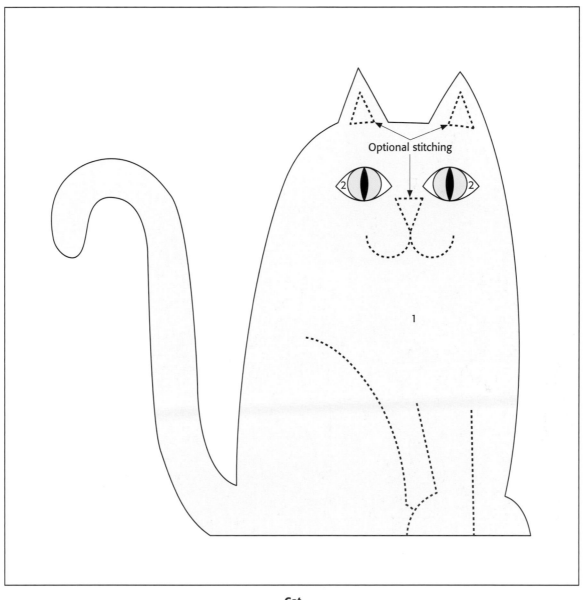

Cat
Enlarge patterns as directed in the project instructions.
Patterns are reversed and do not include seam allowances.

- - - Satin stitch

Optional

Optional

Optional

2

2

2

3

Do not cut tongue for
"Man's Best Friend and
Toys Wall Hanging."

1

Dog
Enlarge patterns as directed in the project instructions.
Patterns are reversed and do not include seam allowances.

- - - Satin stitch

APPLIQUÉ DESIGNS

Fishing
Enlarge patterns as directed in the project instructions.
Patterns are reversed and do not include seam allowances.

- - - Satin stitch
...... Straight stitch

APPLIQUÉ DESIGNS

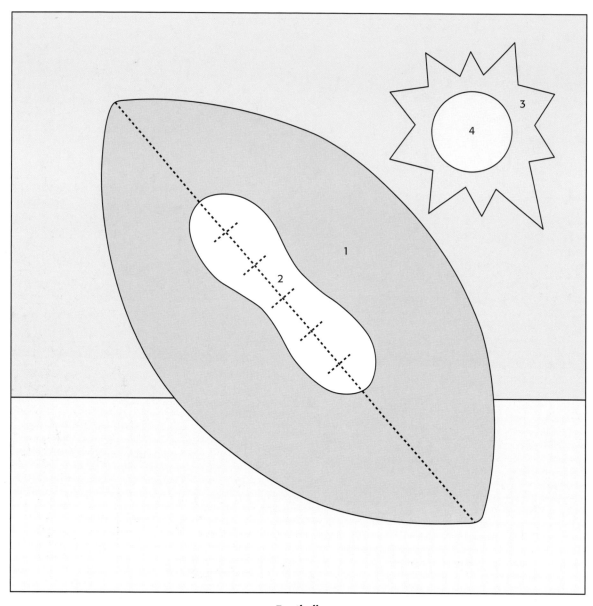

Football
Enlarge patterns as directed in the project instructions.
Patterns are reversed and do not include seam allowances.

--- Satin stitch

APPLIQUÉ DESIGNS

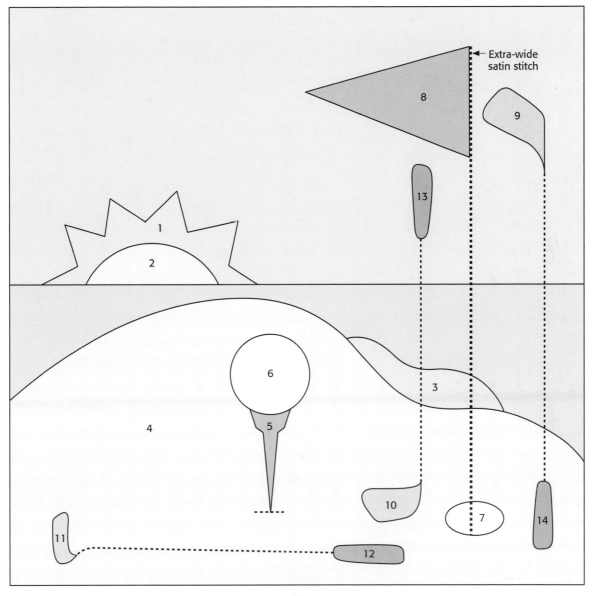

Golfing
Enlarge patterns as directed in the project instructions.
Patterns are reversed and do not include seam allowances.

--- Satin stitch

APPLIQUÉ DESIGNS

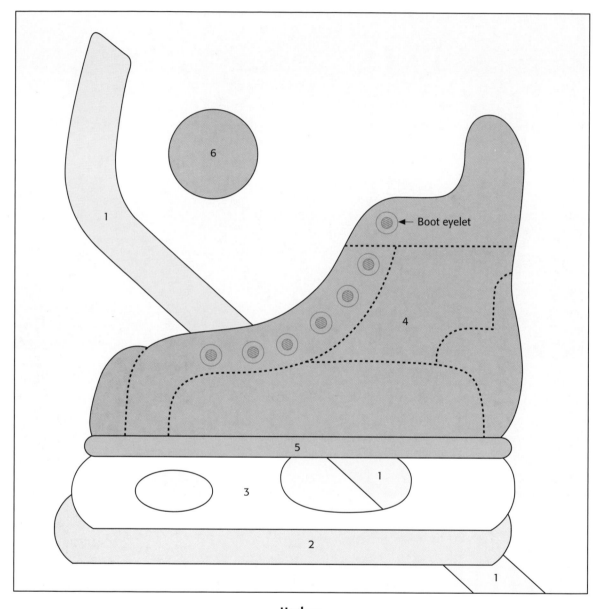

Hockey
Enlarge patterns as directed in the project instructions.
Patterns are reversed and do not include seam allowances.

- - - Satin stitch

APPLIQUÉ DESIGNS

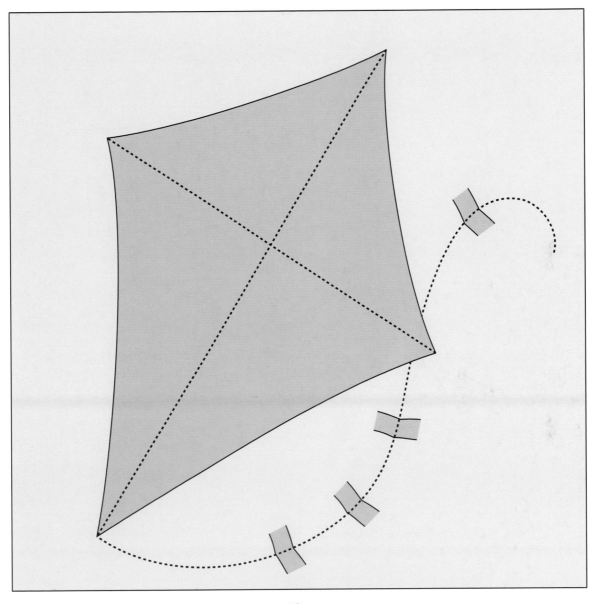

Kite
Enlarge patterns as directed in the project instructions.
Patterns are reversed and do not include seam allowances.

- - - Satin stitch

APPLIQUÉ DESIGNS

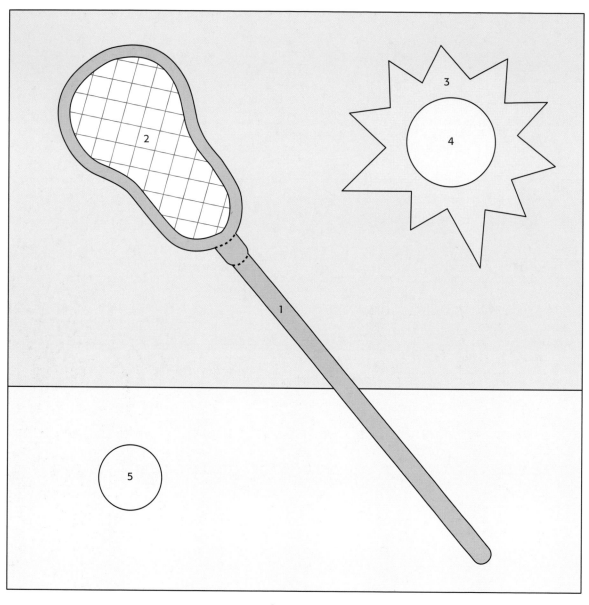

Lacrosse
Enlarge patterns as directed in the project instructions.
Patterns are reversed and do not include seam allowances.

- - - Satin stitch

Motorboat
Enlarge patterns as directed in the project instructions.
Patterns are reversed and do not include seam allowances.

\- - - Satin stitch

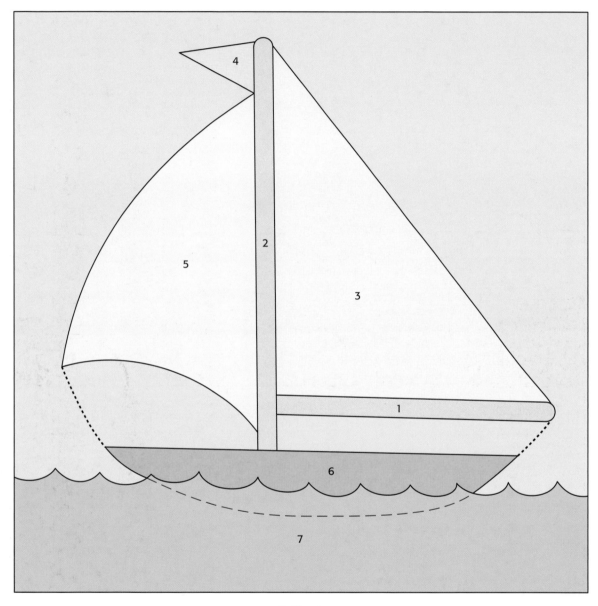

Sailboat
Enlarge patterns as directed in the project instructions.
Patterns are reversed and do not include seam allowances.

- - -   Satin stitch
— —   Use line for bottom of hull for "Little Squirt Quilt."

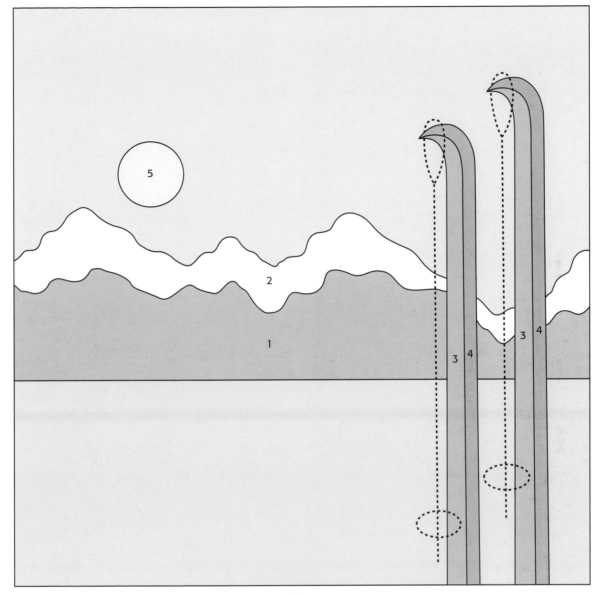

Skiing
Enlarge patterns as directed in the project instructions.
Patterns are reversed and do not include seam allowances.

- - - Satin stitch

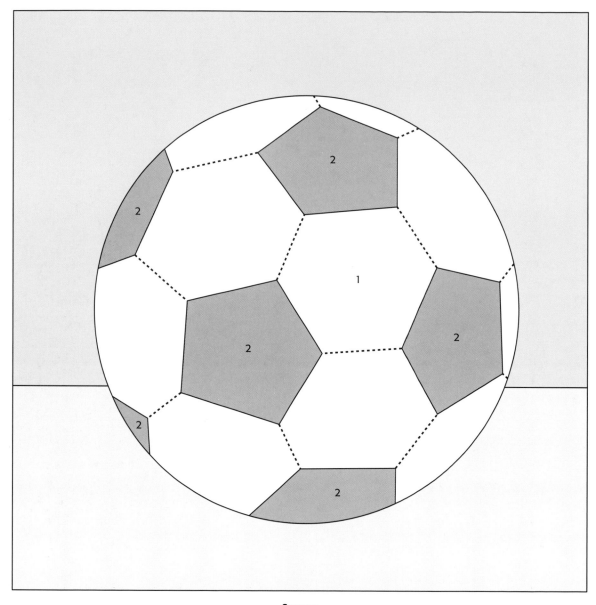

Soccer
Enlarge patterns as directed in the project instructions.
Patterns are reversed and do not include seam allowances.

- - - Satin stitch

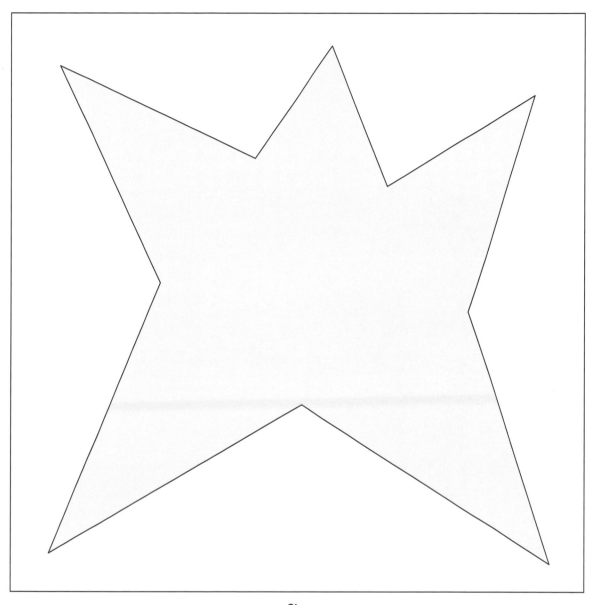

Star
Enlarge pattern as directed in the project instructions.
Pattern is reversed and does not include seam allowance.

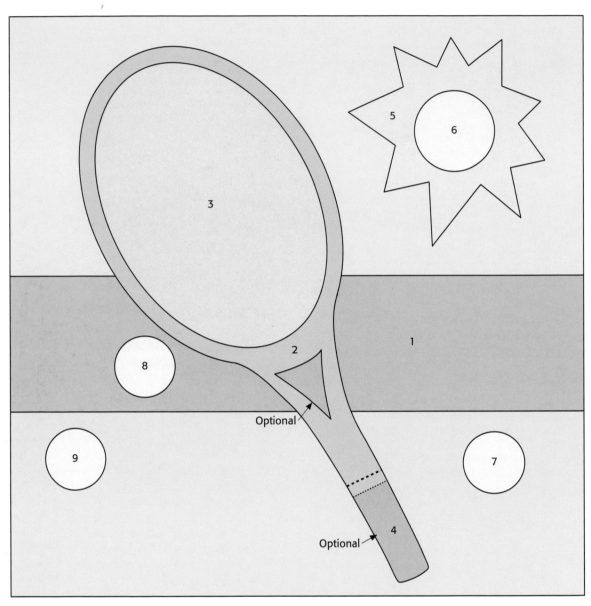

Tennis
Enlarge patterns as directed in the project instructions.
Patterns are reversed and do not include seam allowances.

- - - Satin stitch

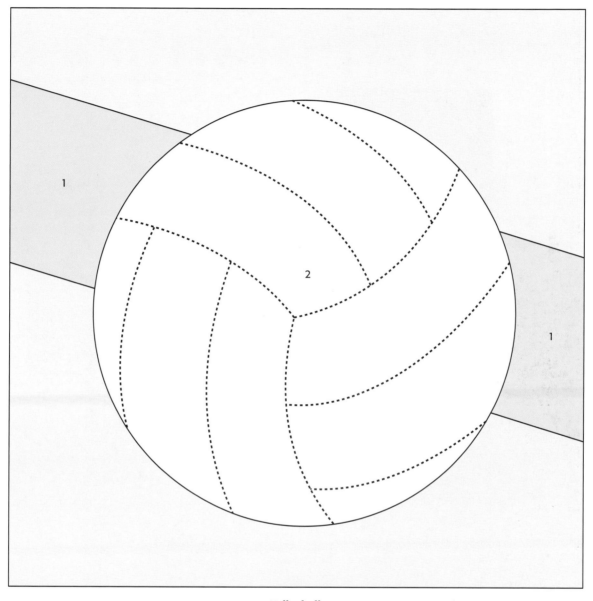

Volleyball
Enlarge patterns as directed in the project instructions.
Patterns are reversed and do not include seam allowances.

-•- Satin stitch

APPLIQUÉ DESIGNS

DeElda Wittmack

has been a fresh influence in the needlework and craft industry for over 35 years. During that time she has had her own needlepoint design business bearing her name. Her designs and unique craft projects have appeared in many magazines—*Better Homes and Gardens, Country Home, Christmas Ideas, Christmas Crafts, Victoria, Ladies' Home Journal*, and *McCall's*, to name a few.

Always a sewer, DeElda began translating her whimsical designs into quilts in 2002. In 2004, she came out with her first quilt line at the International Quilt Market and has been designing and machine-appliqué quilting ever since. She loves the process of turning her pop-art designs into fun and usable quilts and wall hangings for the young and playful at heart. Not the traditional quilter, DeElda uses her home décor projects and patterns that are a little out of the ordinary to lure the younger sewer into the quilt world.

With her two cats and a dog, DeElda lives and works in her home/studio overlooking a small pond in the middle of Iowa. Her greatest accomplishment has been the raising of two grown children—Ellen and Charlie. When she isn't designing with fabric, DeElda enjoys writing children's books, sculpting, painting, and traveling. She also finds time to train for marathons, running to benefit the Leukemia and Lymphoma Society. To see more of DeElda's designs, visit her Web site at www.deelda.com.